Interview

With An

American Monk

Dr. Steven Hairfield

INNERCIRCLE PUBLISHING

Interview With An American Monk
Copyright © 2004
Dr. Steven Hairfield

ISBN: 0-9720080-3-9

Cover design by Chad Lilly and Rick LaFerla

Email your questions on metaphysics to Dr. Hairfield at www.innercirclepublishing.com, or at www.hairfield.com. Some questions may be used in our next book in this series.

Want a new life? Think new thoughts
www.innercirclepublishing.com

Interview

With An

American Monk

featuring
Dr. Steven Hairfield

with
Chad Lilly and Rick LaFerla

of

InnerCircle Publishing

edited by

Christian Kamerer

Your mind is the world
www.innercirclepublishing.com

A note to our readers...

Thank you for purchasing a book from InnerCircle Publishing's catalogue of titles. We appreciate your support.

InnerCircle Publishing sells most of its books through author readings, our website, and most importantly, through word of mouth. We are not a big time New York City publisher. We are a group of poets based in northwest Iowa who publish metaphysical poetry to enlighten and bring new awareness to our readers. We would like to say that all the big time bookstore chains carry our books but quite honestly we can't compete with the big boys for bookstore space. So, we concentrate our efforts elsewhere. We like to go directly to our readers.

Visit our website often. We are finding new authors with wonderful messages and we are putting out new titles every month. We hope that you will enjoy InnerCircle's books for many years to come. Tell your friends that enjoy poetry and metaphysics to visit our website:

www.innercirclepublishing.com.

And rather than offer a 25% discount to bookstores, only to be told it isn't enough, we have decided to offer the discount to you, our readers, who would sincerely appreciate it. All you need to do to get the discount is to buy InnerCircle Publishing books directly from our website.

In this way we hope to build an intimate base of readers who own many ICP titles and don't have to pay bookstore prices.

Chad Lilly

Find yourself in the words
www.innercirclepublishing.com

TABLE OF CONTENTS

Are you aware?
www.innercirclepublishing.com

Introduction....

I have been around people with horsepower before. Not the kind that comes with great power or monetary wealth. It is the power that comes with knowing who you are: Self-empowerment.

I had never met an actual Monk trained in monasteries in the East by real lamas, but my path of learning has taken me into some experiences with similar people: Spiritual people. They are consciously on that path by their own choice. We worked at rehabilitating our spiritual abilities, out of the body experiences, and inspecting past lives. We worked at things like understanding God. So, I'm not on totally unfamiliar turf.

I could tell right away that I was in the presence of someone with a special understanding. There was a soft confidence in his eyes, a compassionateness about his demeanor. People are instantly comfortable in his presence. I could feel a power about him. I know that may sound silly, but maybe you have been around someone like this before, someone that left you astounded. Maybe not. If that *is* the case, I feel for you. You are missing out on something really unique.

I could tell that he had full command of something I have been reaching for, something I have been seeking for a long time. It is difficult to explain, difficult to capture, and difficult to hang onto once tasted. But we all want it. It is why we are here in the first place. It's balance.

You know what I'm talking about; the kind of balance that gets you through negative life experiences. It allows you to keep your head when all of those around you are losing theirs. It allows you to base your decisions on objective observation rather than emotional reaction to the present, or past. Observe and act, rather than react. It keeps you on the right path when the baser desires of the ego are trying to get you to follow a different one. Balance.

Indeed, life is a balancing act. And evidently, Monks are Master Jugglers.

The interview was conducted in a hotel room in Cedar Rapids, Iowa. Dr. Hairfield was doing an event at the Unity Church, as well as some private readings for a clientele he has built. Dr. Hairfield has a PhD in Metaphysics as well as a Masters in Religion and Theology, with a Bachelor's degree in Psychology and takes clients in for private intuitive counseling. However, by his own admission, he is more of a "psychic rather than a therapist, yet in a way they are both the same; one is just faster than the other." Which makes his private readings all the more interesting, I'm sure.

Present at the interview were Chad and Stacy Lilly, myself, Dr. Hairfield, and Mark, a student of his that lived nearby. Chad and I had written down some questions to ask, not so much as a guideline, because quite honestly, neither Chad nor I had any idea what we were in for, let alone what to expect. We wrote them down mostly in the hope that we wouldn't look like we didn't know what we were doing. We didn't. But that didn't matter either.

Steven, Dr. Hairfield, has a way of *going with the flow of the present.* He is unabashed in that there is nothing he can be faced with that he cannot directly handle with the right scripture and a proper explanation of the metaphysics of it. It may come off to some as arrogance. When we determine that another is being arrogant, it may simply be that we chose to attempt lowering another to our already existing level of experience. Perhaps. But it is more accurately a high level of confidence in one's own self, one's abilities, one's wisdom, knowledge, and compassion. There is also arrogance coupled with the improper use of will, or ego. I think that is the arrogance we all are thinking of when we speak of arrogance. With Dr. Hairfield, it's different.

You will notice that Steven has an incredible command of scripture. But it's not a command that we normally know of, as in the way the minister of the local church knows scripture. Most of those can quote scripture to you all day long. But, quite honestly and at the risk of sounding arrogant (there's that word again), they don't know the first thing about the Bible. They can't tell you *why* it was written. They can't tell you *what it is,* exactly. They have actually missed the entire point, the message, and the *intent* of scripture.

Then, throw in the fact that the Bible has suffered countless revisions, alterations, and outright omissions of key ancient texts. Well, it is easy to see how the Bible has become not only the best selling book in history, but the most misunderstood as well.

And that is a tragic reality. The most influential book of our time, read by billions, and yet only a handful truly understand the metaphorical and metaphysical meanings.

The Bible, as Dr. Hairfield points out, is a record of the human metaphysical experience while one is incarnate on Earth. It shows us the various stages of learning and awareness that we will, at some point in our lives, be confronted with and will have to successfully deal with in order to *maintain that balance* that keeps us happy. There's that word again. Balance.

But the lessons are heavily enshrouded in parables and metaphors, and the intended meanings have been missed by us for all these centuries. They define the human experience.

For all the light that understanding the Bible could bring us, we continue to walk in darkness.

Not any longer.

Metaphysics has a bad rap in America. I find that odd, since America is the land of the free, and metaphysics is simply a way for a human to free him/herself from certain bondages we experience in life. It does. It could be that metaphysics is viewed as so much hocus-pocus, snake oil, chanting, and has attracted its fair share of charlatans and con men. All of that is merely a lower harmonic of the real thing. That is not metaphysics.

Metaphysics is about the unseen cause of things. It is seeing that cause and the effect in action. It is about digging into your personality and taking control of the facets of your life that you have delegated to your ego. It is about knowing who you are and how you think and feel. It is about tapping into consciousness and becoming aware of that hidden world where all things are caused. It is about achieving a reverence for life and all things living, and living moment by moment reverently. It is gaining respect for your self and others. It is about knowing God.

That is not for everybody. Many people don't even want to hear one thing about God. I respect that. But for those of us who do, that should be respected also. Hopefully, this book will enlighten you or strengthen your confidence in your self. Some of what you read here may be new. Maybe not. It just depends on how much study and meditation you have put into these subjects.

Many people think that living a reverent life means a life of abstaining from everything you think is fun now. That is not the case. You can be a reverently studious person and still have plenty of fun. In fact, you might have even more fun living that way. Until it has been experienced, you wouldn't know. But people have preconceived ideas about what living in reverence means.

Metaphysics may have also gained this reputation because, quite frankly, not very many people have the patience to invest themselves into this study enough to get the end result of full understanding. They get burdened with too many misunderstood concepts and give up on it.

We've thrown it into the same basket as black or white magic, mysticism, ESP, out of the body experiences, past lives, karma, and all the rest, and we call it "stuff that can't be proven so it isn't worthy of my attention." If we can't see it with our eyes, feel it with our fingers, smell it, taste it, or hear it scream when we kill it, it isn't real.

But there it is, still there.

Metaphysics is not difficult to understand. It is probably harder to accept it as real and true than it is to understand it. That's because you can't see metaphysics with your physical eyes. You see it with your spiritual senses. Your eyes only capture the physicality, but what you see had already been created, so by the time you see it, there is nothing you can do to change it. Metaphysics takes you to that place where things are caused before they are seen. That is another dimension. That is what is "behind the veil." When you can be there, you will be in the place where the manifestation you see with your eyes here is first created.

It can be a hard subject to study because it flies right into the teeth of what you think you know and believe. That is a healthy thing, if you allow it to happen, because it will strip away the false ideas you have been trying to compute with for your entire life. The falsehoods peel off layer by layer leaving you caught in one epiphany after another. It can leave you speechless, breathless.

And then you look at Dr. Hairfield, and it was all explained in a very matter-of-fact manner. The only hint of excitement detectable to me was a bright light in the center of his easy, brown eyes. He loves what he is doing. That is easy to see.

So, if you are ready for change, read on. If you are ready for challenge, read on. If you are ready to open the inner world of the real you, read on.

And may you never be the same again.

Chad Lilly and Rick LaFerla

Part I:

Early Zen teachings

and….

"I've lived how many times?"

The following text is transcribed directly from audio tape. We wanted it to be original, not edited down to a watery likeness of the real thing. You are getting it "straight from the horse's mouth."

We pick up the conversation as Chad Lilly was discussing one of Inner Circle Publishing's recent books, written by Kirstie Silk.

Chad: She's an Australian and she's got some interesting things to say. It's on a different level, as far as, how do you say it, not on a simpler level, but she's expressing the exact same message. Different words, you know?

Rick: Different words. Different experience. The more ways you say it you're going to reach more people, I think.

Steven: I think the whole world's in a real transition phase right now, which is why we're seeing the struggle and the turmoil. Humans don't change easily. And when they do change, we struggle with it before we actually accomplish the shift. Christ Himself said that you cannot put new wine in old skins, and I feel in reality, this is what we are still attempting to do. I believe the whole world is headed toward consciousness. And it's the majority of the churches, it's the governments that are all losing out, and I think they know it. They want to keep people intimidated and somewhat frightened, and of course get the money generally under false pretenses.

You know, they've got us so used to reliance on government as a form of protection. I mean, if the economy were to collapse, you think the government would help you? Is the municipality going to help you?

Chad: They are going to help you in the sense that they will wheel the National Guard in.

Steven: To protect you from you?

Chad: To protect me from my neighbor who's as hungry as I am. To protect the starving people from each other perhaps.

Steven: I was watching CNN this morning. Some of the Democratic stuff. The Democrats were talking about New Hampshire, and how one of them, Edwards, said that the American people need us, the politicians, to define what the idea of "extremism" means. I sat there (laughing) and I looked at the TV and I went, "What?" That's what I mean by government. They set up the definitions and most people swallow it. And they go along with it. I mean, if you really think about it, the last thing that any of these institutions want is free thinkers. They're afraid of you.

Chad: That's right.

Steven: They are absolutely afraid of you all, because you don't conform.

Rick: I've sent a couple emails to Oprah for you. I've sent a couple emails to NPR, Coast to Coast. I sent one to Montel Williams too.

Chad: If you'd get on Oprah, it would be....

Steven: I've had the opportunity to be on radio and T.V. shows. I can get a little outspoken, very forward, as there is only truth to be concerned with and that, at all times, is not personal truth. It is simply just truth. I can get real esoteric at the same time.

Rick: I think you have a range to work on any of those programs. Gary Zukav. I saw Gary Zukav when he was on Oprah. And ah, you know, his message is very much similar to yours. You know?

Steven: Well, we're all saying the same things, like you said. Different take on the same subject. It's that consciousness thing coming alive, and we are all inseparably connected to it. We just use it more than most.

Rick: Yeah, that was when *The Seat of the Soul* had been out for, I don't know, a year or so, and *Heart of the Soul* had just broke and he was on there promoting that. But of course, Oprah had read *Seat of the Soul* and they talked a lot about that book and stuff like that. That was a good little book.

Chad: (To Rick.) Did you want to do some of your questions?

Rick: Um, yeah, we'll get to them.

Chad: Because we were talking about doing this and putting it up on the site. And we thought of real questions.

Rick: I've got some questions for you.

Chad: ....and come up with some questions....

Rick: I told Chad, I said "I'm going to beat him up (Laughter). I'm going to put him up on the wall, man" (Everyone laughing.)

Steven: Mark was at the meeting for the radio show that night. Because Mary, that's in California, Mary Suhr, she likes to have a plan. And I told Terry when we were having dinner, because he said, "What's our plan for the night?" And I said, "Our plan is having no plan. I'm just going with the flow, whatever comes let's do it."

And he looked at me and laughed and said, "You know, Mary.." Yeah. So we go in the conference room, get a conference call going.

And she calls in at the pre-designated time and Mary says, "What are we doing?" And I say, "I don't know. Whatever you want to do." "Steven, you're the one on the show." "I know. What do you want?" I said, "You guys know me by now. Let's just wing it." Where I'm going is, the live questions from you, Terry and the listeners, and as you know, I like that. I get to interface with consciousness and the answers will flow from there.

Chad: Oh.

Steven: I mean, you heard them (referring to some people who called into a radio show he did in January.) Even that guy Michael that called in. We got into quantum physics. Actually, I'm going for another PhD in quantum theory.

Chad, Rick, Stacy: Really, wow.

Steven: I understand it anyway. You know, I do.

Rick: Yeah, but it needs to be broken down. You know that's one thing Zukav did, pretty well I thought, was breaking quantum physics down into more...

Steven: It's more like sacred geometry.

Rick: Exactly. There is a sacredness about it and it needs to be broken down into metaphysical terms and applied to, you know, a real person, in layman's terms.

Steven: Everybody...

Rick: (Laughing.) I hate that phrase.

Steven: Everybody... Actually, you are right, because when you came on the radio show, that's one of the things you said, was that - meaning simplicity. And I thought to myself, "Yeah, he's right." Because I think too many people get out there on this spiritual road; they get out there talking and they make it so darn complex.

Rick: Plus too, people shouldn't be looking into this subject for an interest in outer space. Let's bring it all back into here (pointing at the heart) where it belongs. Where it really is.

Steven: That's esoteric, not exoteric.

Rick: Yeah.

Rick: One of the questions I had was how many years were you trained in the monasteries?

Steven: A total of six, but in reality, my whole life is lived from that concept.

Rick: Okay.

Steven: Between several different ones. Primarily it was Tibetan and Zen, actually. All of it comes out of India originally. Bodhi Dharma, who is the founder of Zen, actually came out of India and went into China. And Bodhi Dharma, actually if you were to put it in layman's terms, is "embodied path" is what that stands for. Dharma meaning path, bodhi is the reference to the material. So, that's actually what that phrase stands for. I spent about a year and a half with them. And I was with the yogis and a few Hindu ascetics in India.

Rick: How old were you at the time?

Steven: I began at 18. At eighteen I was in a combat zone and I guess in a way its kind of like seeing the movies. My CO liked me. He knew I could accomplish the task. And when I was back in base camp I was actually over at the Zen monastery in Quang Ngai. So at 18, I was in a combat zone and in a Zen monastery at the same time.

Rick: Unbelievable.

Steven: And then I went to college for the first time ...Yeah, that's what it is. (Laughing, referring to Rick's comment.) You have to learn to balance those opposites.

Rick: Yeah, exactly.

Steven: All of life is masculine and feminine energy that we are to use in union, one with the other, not in opposition, as we do it at present.

Rick: Yeah.

Steven: And religion has it all goofed up. Because in the Book of Genesis, it says that God created the two luminaries. Well, what It created was the masculine energy and the feminine energy, and the rest was created from that. Night is actually feminine, daylight is masculine. You know, if you were to really break it down into a metaphysical sense. After I got my Bachelor's degree in psychology, I knew they didn't necessarily know their head from a hole in the ground. And I had this urge to go to India. Should I tell them that story? (To Mark.)

Mark: Yeah.

Steven: The last six months I was in college I had this just overwhelming urge to go to India. Now I had never been there. And the Zens had taught me to always follow your impulses or urges, that inner guidance system. If you have an urge and it wants you to do a thing or something you're going to learn, so just go do it.

And by the time I was approaching June graduation, May actually, I couldn't stand it anymore. So I knew…I just had all my finals….I didn't even wait around for graduation, the caps and all that celebration stuff. I just sold all my stuff, pooled the money, put what I had left in a pack and jumped on a jet, and I flew to India. And I'm stomping around through India wondering what in the daylights am I doing in this place?

But my impulses kept taking me north, up towards the Punjab where the deserts of northern India are. And I wanted some tea, so I sat down in this little roadside shanty, and was drinking some tea and looking out at this dirt road. And I got into watching the dust swirl behind the carts and wasn't paying any attention, and all of a sudden this voice behind me said, "We've been waiting for you." (Everyone laughs.)

Still watching the dust and the people and ...wow. And the voice again said something, but this time what it said was, "Your name is Steven, is it not?"

The first thing I did was look around for Rod Serling. (Everyone laughs.) Thought I was in the Twilight Zone. And I turned around and it was the softest brown eyes I'd ever seen in my life.

And it was another Monk. And I looked at him and I said, "Yes, my name is Steven, how did you know?"

And he said, "We've been waiting for you."

And I said, "How did you know I was going to be here?"

And he looked at me and smiled and said, "You have much to learn, but we began calling for you six months ago and we knew that you would be here on this day, at this time, and we came to greet you."

And that's when I got my first lesson about what consciousness really is. Later I learned how it operates and to operate within it. The truth is, we all do, but we do not necessarily realize it.

Rick: Yeah, what an eye opener. I bet you were hooked after that.

Steven: Well, certainly. The next thing he said, like you guys I'm American, and my entire... aside from the experience with the Zens, my entire analytical nature had just been rocked to the core. And monks are known to do that. They'd rather rock you.

Chad: I think that's healthy.

Rick: I do too.

Steven: It is.

Rick: I do too. Shake me up. Crack open my cranium and mix it up.

Steven: I looked at him and said, "What do you mean I'm here to learn?" or that I have a lot to learn.

He said, "You're here to learn about Issa."

And I said, "Who's Issa?"

And he said, "That's the one you know as Jesus. He was here."

And I simply said…what? So now he had my full attention.

And I laughed and said, "Okay I've got a few weeks." And it turned into many years. But those guys made darn sure that I had an education that I don't think you can touch anywhere.

Rick: Oh, I agree. This is why I'm so interested in it, because once I got to understand your background, you've done all the stuff I wanted to do.

Steven: Why didn't you do it?

Rick: I just, you know… fear, mostly.

Steven: The Zens would tell you that your three greatest teachers are what you fear, what you avoid, and what you deny. Go towards those things.

Rick: Yeah.

Steven: I mean, if it's going to hurt you physically you will know it. Don't go with that. What we term as God is more the Creative

Principle, and it truly has no desire to hurt you, no matter what the fundamentalists say.

Rick: Right.

Steven: But if it's a fear... ego is a thing that wants you to grow old, it wants you to get sick, it wants you to die, it wants you to fail. And your ego is the thing that will present what you fear, what you avoid and what you deny to you. If your own soul mate or more precisely your twin flame, is coming in your direction, your ego will want you to avoid and go another way. So, if you follow what you avoid, you will meet that soul mate. Of course, a soul mate can be good news and bad news.

Chad: Yeah.

Steven: In reincarnation, the average is between 200 and 250 times. So, some of those soul mates can be somebody you have fought hundreds of times in other lifetimes. So again, if you go toward that, you would learn about yourself and soon there are no fears to speak of.

Rick: So there could be more than one soul mate.

Steven: Oh, you bet. It's more of what people really are saying. When they say soul mate, they are really looking for their twin vibration, their twin flame - not necessarily a soul mate. Soul mate, there is a connection too, of course, but this can be a multitude of things and not necessarily the true love of your life.

Rick: But not like a twin flame.

Steven: No.

Rick: A soul mate could be into your life to cause you all kinds of hell and havoc for the lesson to be learned there? Is that the case? Or not?

Steven: Well, in the Bible, Yeshua himself says that. How does he actually phrase it, "Not one jot nor one tittle shall pass until all things are balanced."

That's karma. He's talking about the same thing that Buddha was talking about in the idea of karma. Karma's not a form of punishment like we think it. It is a balancing of sorts, a weighing of the scales to assure balance. If you murder someone...

Rick: (Laughing.) Sure feels like it sometimes.

Steven: Zens talk about mindfulness. Intention in life. What is your intention. If you steal.... Take an example, a couple that's married and one of them has an affair. The one that has an affair, the karmic repercussion is now: how can you trust your partner?

Chad: That's right.

Steven: That's the karmic repercussion.

Rick: Yeah, because "I did it."

Steven: Okay. A person that steals is going to be stolen from. That's the way it works. You murder someone, that person is going to incarnate in another lifetime *with you,* and you may be born on the other side of the world from each other, but I can promise you...

Rick: You're going to get your payback.

Steven: Yes. Yes.

Chad: What goes around...

Steven: But the object is to not. Let's say they murdered you and the karmic balance this time is to...

Rick: Balance it off.

Steven: The way is to be above it by not giving into it. The ideal is to always be at peace within you, and your life can only reflect that back to you. This is the key. You want love, then love you. When a person is able to see only perfection, then that is all there is, simply perfection constantly in a state of unfolding.

Rick: Get off the wheel by not going...

Steven: Encountering. Let them do what they are going to do, and walk away.

Rick: And walk away. I agree.

Steven: You guys know who the ascended masters are? There are twelve of these masters. There's Meitreya. El Morya. The one that fascinates me is Djwal Khul. He was a Chinese warrior, back in the days when they were tribal, basically, and how he became a master as he met his archenemy on the field of combat. He had his troops. His enemy had their troops. They fought their way to each other. And Khul had this guy, had him down on his knees without a sword. Had his hair in his hand and was holding his head up and drew his sword back, and of course, both factions stopped.

And the two leaders came together. And Khul looked at him, threw his sword down and he says, "No, this ceases here." And he stopped. And of course everybody looked at him like their boss had just blown his cookies, had just lost it. And he turned around and he lectured both sides about combat and the evilness of combat. And you know those two guys became allies? Khul wouldn't fight, but if it was necessary he would for him?

Chad: Right.

Steven: So his karmic circumstance was broken, and that's the very thing that got Khul into his mastership. It was that very act alone, because he could have perpetuated it and he chose not to at that one moment in time. He transmuted all energetic debt and became a warrior of the universe, a war without the need to kill. We all could perpetuate anything, whether peace, love, compassion or war, it does not matter because it is the creation in the moment that creates the future energetic payback. And it's always within our own hands to change it at any given moment. See, I'm a dangerous guy to ask a question of.

Rick: That's right. I love it. You mentioned Meitreya. What can you tell us about him?

Steven: Well, he's supposed to be the next Buddha. Energy point coming in. In fact you could even say the next Christ. It's an energy point or a return of a specific consciousness level into physical form which we term as human, but more advanced than before. This advance is because of the higher level of ability of comprehension of, say, our present era.

Rick: Has he not appeared yet?

Steven: I can answer that one. Yes, he's on earth.

Chad: In human form?

Steven: Yes. But it can form itself into a human and be a human. Once every 2,000 years. But he is here, as it has been 2,000 years since the last appearance.

Steven: Let's understand something. The reason Christ, in theory, had happen to him what happened to him was not because of who he was. It was because of his seeming arrogance, and his perceived ego.

A powerful human is going to come across to everybody else as one egotistical human being, because they will bow to no one. So, whether they are egocentric or not, only they themselves will know, and most large egos don't recognize it anyway. So you still have the push and shove, especially if we come fromposition of dominance or one that needs to be in control. That was not Christ's issue; it was those in fear of losing their control.

Part II:

500 year old Monks,

out in infinity, and....

"Who said I couldn't walk on water?"

Rick: On the ShadowWorlds program, you mentioned you were trained by monks that were three to five hundred years old.

Steven:(Laughing.) Um hmm.

Rick: Tell us about that.

Steven:(Laughing) Anything that happens in that part of the world, the American mind is going to have the propensity to question. And I must say that is merely a guesstimate and not known, for they do not necessarily celebrate age as we do. Time to a monk, for the most part, is irrelevant as they learn to always be in the present, which means the past and the future are not important, other than what they create in the moment and shows as a future event when timing occurs.

Rick: Sure.

Steven: Physiologically, medical science can tell you there is no reason for aging. But we do. Why? Mind. Mind stuff. We think too much and we, in this part of the world, are always analyzing, especially previous events.

When you learn how to focus the mind.... In fact, the excerpt right in the very front of this book is right out of the Essene Gospel of Peace.

And it says, "Only the sons of Men is it given the power of thought. Even that thought can break the bonds of death."

And that was written originally about two (thousand) to 2500 years ago. They knew it then. And if you look at who begot who in the Bible, even Methuselah lived, according to the Bible, 997 years. Adam lived 995.

Rick: Yeah, but they question the calendar year and all of that jazz.

Steven: Well, modern science wants physical proof for spiritual things. We also must remember that all calendars have been changed on many occasions; besides it is not truly about how long we live as much as it is about what we do with the time that we have.

Rick: Right, yeah.

Steven: ....and you're not going to get it most times from looking for physical proof. In Corinthians, Paul says that we should walk in faith and not by what the eye sees, and here at times is where science falls through the cracks. If we thought about it, there is no direct proof of God unless we know how to perceive and not just look. The missing link is more a spiritual thing and not a physical thing.

Rick: No, you're not going to get it if we do not apply metaphysics into the equation.

Steven: If you knew within you, with no doubt and no question, called faith, that you aren't going to die and you allowed, through the proper focused life, you allowed your body to be what it is and be in total acceptance of that body, there is no logical or illogical reason for death. Either that, or all the Ancients are not telling us the truth.

Rick: (Laughing.) Right. Exactly.

Steven: We get caught up in age limitation created by birthdays and what medical science says. But if we look at the progression, going by history, the average age used to be about 55 to 60 years old when they met their transition. Today you are looking at 75 to even 85 and some geneticists now say that if you hear this, the average lifespan you will see achieve 125 to 150 years old. It's already taking place.

But if you understand the makeup of the body/mind relationship, you and I had this conversation on the phone initially, your body—18 months from today— will not have a cell in it that's here today. Some of it regenerates faster than that. The eye, 24 hours. The lungs, 24 hours. I mean that's a total regeneration.

If we're living properly within ourselves, in full acceptance of ourselves, then your cells are constantly regenerating in a state of absolute pure perfection. Perfection has no end result other than creating further perfection. There are some authors out there today that say God is perfect and it created imperfection. This begs the question: How could perfection create imperfection?

And if you also take a look at the Biblical text that say you are made in the image and likeness, well now you're saying God's going to die.

No, It doesn't.

That image and likeness actually means, as Yeshua himself said in the Book of John, that you are God. That's who you are. You know. Why destroy yourself? You do that not so much by what you put in you, as even He stated. It's what you put out in your expression which will destroy you. I mean, where that story actually came from was because of an older monk that I used to run with, every Saturday and Sunday during my studies there. There was a period of time where I liked to jog. And during the week, I would run on the average of five miles a day. On a Saturday or Sunday I would run greater distances about 25 miles. Now understand that was at 9,000 to 13,000 feet.

Chad: Yeah.

Steven: And on Saturday and Sunday I would do 25 miles. About, say 25,000. (Chuckles.) I would have run all the way to the States. (Everyone laughs.)

And every Saturday and Sunday, and I never knew until that morning that that's the day I was going to do it. And every single time, when I walked out of the monastery, there he was. This elderly Monk. And I asked him, one day when we were doing a cool down coming back after 25 miles, I looked at him and said, "How old are you, Master?"

And he said, "I don't know. We don't track birthdays like you do."

You don't know how old you are? And he started pointing out things he remembered, going all the way back to World War I. And this was in the seventies? All right. And looking at the guy, you could not tell how old he was. There wasn't a wrinkle on his face. Nothing. But the thing that got me is when I got to the human door and opened it and I turned around and looked, and he was gone.

Chad: The human door?

Steven: Yeah, well there's a big gate so you can drive vehicles in and there's another door. I didn't want to call it a "man door." (Everybody laughs.)

Steven: And when I turned around he was gone. But you also have to understand...have you ever read The Teachings of the Masters of the Far East?

Everybody: No.

Steven: That stuff actually happens, and we in this part of the world think that it is flights of fancy. No, it is very real as any limitation occurs because of our own mental conditioning, and we apply the limitation through what we come to believe as a fact.

Rick: I've always felt in my gut that it was all true.

Steven: It is.

Rick: Yeah.

Mark: Once you read *Masters of the Far East*, everything else is just a repeat. Don't you think? (To Steven.)

Steven: Yeah. There are Monks. There are Neophytes, which are new travelers. And then there are Monks, which means they're genuine. And then, there are Masters. And then there are Adepts. Those are the people you want to know. This reminds me of an ancient Chinese proverb that says: do not seek the wise for what they know, but seek what they sought. This means: make the journey yourself and look for yourself. This is the only way, and it comes through the experience, not just the written word. This is the error in this part of the world. We merely intellectualize it and not necessarily get the experience of it.

Rick: The Adepts?

Steven: Yes, because they do whatever they choose.

Rick: So they understand energy manipulation.

Steven: Absolutely.

Rick: Mocking and unmocking the body.

Steven: Um hmm.

Rick: Placing it in another place. Mocking it up.

Steven: Absolutely.

Rick: That's incredible.

Steven: I remember Master Lobsang, because he knew my

31

curiosity about energy manipulation. And he looked at me and said, "Well, we'll have a Nath yogi come." Well, the Naths, if you go into India and you ask about a Nath, nobody will know what the heck you are talking about. They've been around for thousands of years. And they are the true adepts. They will find you if they consider you worthy and that you will not abuse the knowledge. In reality, you cannot anyway.

Rick: But nobody knows them.

Steven: (Grins.) Ah, oh, yeah.

Rick: I would imagine. If you were an Adept wouldn't you want to be kind of undercover? (Laughing.)

Steven: I was working in a field one day, and a shadow was cast over me and I looked up, and it was this "scrungy" older gentleman. And I looked at him and kind of went, (mimics a look.)

And he was standing there, still looking at me. And all of a sudden he spits and he says, "You no good. You no can do."

And he turned around and walked away. And I went: what in the daylights was that about? And this went on for about two, two and a half weeks. This old man would show up. And each time he would show up and it was on a regular schedule. And he was just there seemingly from nowhere.

And then, after this time span, one day he asked me why I wanted to learn. And I told him about the connection I had with the Jesus energy. The idea of all that.

He nodded and he goes, "But you're an American. You're just so full of your own self."

There was no way. And I didn't see the guy for two weeks after the questions. Forgot all about it. Two weeks later I'm out in the field, and I get a tap on the shoulder. And I turn around and it's him. And he looked at me and said, "Come with me."

So, as we were walking, I begun talking with him and, of course, he didn't want to answer me. He asked for silence, for to him, I was disturbing the universe with my chatter. But finally it was basically realized that he had been testing me to see if I would be the typical American and lose it. And the only reason that he ultimately invited me was because he knew I was serious and my energy felt right to him, as he put it. That's when I saw some amazing and mind boggling events that totally defied logic, that's metaphysics for you.

Rick: Cool.

Chad: What kind of amazing things?

Steven: Ohhh…heavens to Betsy. Are you going to put this in there?

Rick: We don't have to if you don't want to.

Chad: We can turn it off if you want.

Rick: You can have us censure anything you don't feel right about. It's fine.

Steven: How about people appearing and disappearing?

Rick: Cool.

Steven: Nobody ever cooking but having warm food that just appears.

Rick: Cool.

Steven: No house. You turn around, it's there.

Rick: (Laughing.) I love it.

Steven: Every human has that power.

Rick: Yeah. See, now why would you need anything if you had that power actualized?

Steven: Why do you think society went the way that it did? Because if everybody knew what Jesus was taught, which, when you read the revision in Parable, you will see why. Most Churches would never have a footing, but God consciousness would. Governments also would have to be changed along with it, and too many people and organizations would lose their power over the masses.

Rick: The enslavers need slaves.

Steven: Exactly, and to think all Masters through the eons have taught equality in an absolute sense. What we don't realize about the Inquisition or what was really going on behind the scenes, is they were hunting those people. That's who they were killing, it's the people that... who not only could do it, but were teaching others how to do it.

Chad: Sure.

Rick: Wow.

Chad: That almost answers the question: what is it that keeps a person who is interested awake? Faith.

Steven: One of the things I challenge people to do all of the time is when you think something, watch in front of you. Just simply watch in front of you. The biggest hints of this happen to still be within the Biblical text amongst others, and the key is to not interpret to a material sense. Leave it spiritual or metaphysical. You have to keep your eyes single. You have to be single in purpose, one hundred per cent of the time. You can't serve two masters. "I can't see this, so I don't know if I can trust that." This is what most people process in the mental sense and this is not faith, this is doubt.

Chad: Yeah, yeah.

Steven: And you repeatedly have to take a leap of faith. You repeatedly, constantly; it's like some of the... when Jesus is asked in the Book of Matthew, "Master, how do you pray?" there is something that was edited out. How do we know that? Because I read the original texts. Because of the Tibetans. What he said was: you must know that you have the thing before the thing is ever given you. And therein lies the key.

See, we work for money. That's what human condition has led it to. We work for power and control. And therein lies the delusion. Therein lies the difficulty that you, Mark, or Rick, being an adept, or Stacy, forgive me, being an adept, there's nothing that stops you, except you and the present state of mind the average person lives with.

Buddha said it. Krishna said it. Zoroster, Zarathustra, they all said it. You're born empowered. You're born perfect. You're born enlightened. And you spend the rest of your life getting away from it, until you hit that wall. Where you go, there's got to be something different. And then you look.

Chad: I'm looking.

Steven: Where are you looking?

Chad: Inside. I'm listening. I'm hearing. I feel like I can see. But there are some things where you don't always trust it. Things like that. But if you're working on it... still doesn't seem as if...

Steven: You knew that they exist; you've just never gone to find it for yourself. The universe is funny because when you truly begin to search, it will lead the way or take you to what you wish to know. The example is simple: you have been seeking, and here I am so to speak for parts of your answers. But if you don't follow your impulses, you don't follow your urges, what good is having the realization that you are totally empowered?

Chad: Right.

Steven: I wonder what the world's going to do when the big quantum theory proves out what every Master has said throughout time?

Chad: What? They will mathematically....

Steven: ....prove it? Yes.

Chad: Prove it?

Steven: Sure.

Chad: Get it on paper?

Steven: They are already getting there. They are already getting there.

Rick: I'm sure they will be able to.

Steven: Oh! Sure, they will. I mean quantum theory has now really pushed the walls of the mind beyond present comprehension.

Rick: There's just got to be a mathematical equation to this whole....thing.

Steven: ....the whole reason of your life is because...ponder this: if you didn't have touch, smell, sight, sound...

Chad: Sensory input.

Steven: Yeah…how would your mind work?

Chad: The mind is totally capable of all information, why would it need some sort of…

Steven: Ahhh… it would need to define what it wanted to accomplish. Before we had bodies, you could almost say God was absolutely naïve or unintelligent. What kind of experience would It have had?

Rick: You'd…you'd have to.

Steven: How did It know?

Rick: It had no experience. Yeah.

Steven: So, pardon the pun, the "soul" reason for the creation of the body was to attain experience. So It would have knowledge, wisdom, not theory.

If people took one word, "infinite," we know that mathematically. But do we intellectually understand infinity? We don't experience it because we live in mental confinement and keep ourselves away from pure oneness with all things.

When we enter consciousness and you get that buzz, you are part of infinity. That's what that is. So what we've done through the eons, intentionally, is we've gone from infinite to finite so that we know how to operate in infinite on return. And you see that cycle in the Biblical text, twice, or actually three times, and we are headed to the fourth. Right now. And only those that are able to wield it will be able to reach higher….. Did you ever see *What Dreams May Come*?

Everybody: Oh yes.

37

Steven: That's so close to the truth that it's not even funny.

Rick: I thought it was too.

Steven: That we can do what's on the other side, here and now. And the purpose is to do what we do on the other side here. I mean on the other side, to hug is not even really possible as we understand it, because the body is finer or what we could term as higher vibration, and all life is vibration by its very nature. You know, it's like...um...

Chad: Unnecessary?

Steven:...well, I don't know if there is anything necessary or unnecessary. But the whole object of physical form is to give definition, but not confinement as we are prone to do.

Chad: Right.

Steven: We've become locked in that.

Chad: But when you're one, who can you hug? (General laughter.)

Chad: That's what I'm saying, it's unnecessary, you're touching all things.

Steven: Okay, I would buy that.

Chad: (Laughing.)

Steven: From that point of view, and again, that's the very thing that limits people from their God-given, natural, "Adept-ship". Because we think we cannot. The first time I walked on water, I had a monk on each side of me but, boy, talk about blow your mind.

Chad: Yeah.

Steven: It's like you're standing there, telling each other, "We can't do this."

Chad: Right.

Steven: So, I can state that I had a Peter experience. As long as Christ had him, he could stand on the water. As soon as He let go of him, his own doubt ate him up. And there's no faith there and you have the reality of inner division showing in the outer world.

So, if you understand the idea of infinity, then you already know right off the bat everything is infinite. In scope, as far out as it can go - as far in as it can go also. And you can operate in that playing field. That tree can't (pointing out the window.) That tree can't. That dog or that ant can't. But the funny thing is they operate under one principle. We don't. We do, but we don't use it. And if we understand the idea of infinity, then death isn't even possible.

Rick: Absolutely true. That's what finally put me there too. When you were a student in the monasteries, what was a typical day like?

Steven: Oh wow. It was never the same. Never routine.

Rick: Okay.

Steven: Um…my favorite thing was, when I was a Zen, was the Zen garden. The sand in the Zen garden is the stuff that we know that we can change and it changes very fluidly.

The smaller rocks are the things that we know that we can influence and create change with, but are a little bit of work, and here is where we, as the human, begin to falter and hesitate and tend to become confused because of the unknown.

The boulders, which took 3, 4, 5, 10 monks to move, were things we totally resist and refuse to change. So, that's the symbolism of the Zen garden. When I was with the Zens, that was my first love right there, because I always went after those huge boulders.

Rick: Um hmm.

Steven: Big suckers. To rearrange their place took much effort, but [it] gave the greatest reward.

To a Tibetan, that could vary as the day. You could be assigned, I mean everybody has duties. You have cooks. You have people that clean. One of my favorite things with them was every monk, once you attained the status of a monk, you have a candle lit for you. And that candle burns forever. And what you do is, at night, you always have several monks going through the monastery making sure no candle ever goes out. And when it gets to a certain size you light a new one, remove the old one, blow it out, and put the new one in its place. So it burns perpetually.

Rick: Cool.

Steven: That was a cool thing.

But you could be gardening or getting ready to start a function, and one of the masters comes up to you and says, "Walk with me."

And you know you're about to get a whale of a lesson.

You ultimately learn to meditate 24/7. You have your meditation chambers where you do it as a group. And they teach you moving meditations, walking meditations. The idea is to get into perpetual consciousness and stay there. So, anything that takes you toward that point is what you do.

Rick: Right.

Steven: Get attacked by tigers, whatever. (All laugh.)

Rick: Cool. So you mentioned that you walked on water. What other types of things have you done like that?

Steven: Lit a room.

Rick: Lit a room?

Steven: Um hmm.

Rick: Just go into a dark room and your presence lights it?

Steven: Um hmm.

Rick: That's cool.

Steven: Yeah. We don't need this stuff (lights.)

Rick: Huh uh. What's the secret behind those things?

Steven: Higher vibration. You generate any vibration you choose by the state of mind...

Rick: So how does a being generate that? Do you just think it? Concentrate on it?

Steven: Image it.

Rick: Imagery.

Steven: Yes. The mind doesn't think in words. It thinks in pictures. In imagery.

Part III:

"Who is thinking that?"

And....

"God is what?"

Rick: Well, this takes me to a question that this is the perfect time to ask it. What's your plan for the future? What is it you are trying to accomplish?

Steven: Ah... I don't know. Kinda tough to answer that one.

Rick: Okay. I thought you might be working towards a particular goal.

Steven: I have a mission, yeah. I have a mission.

Rick: Can you share it?

Steven: Sure. But future is, I mean that's about as irrelevant as the thing that we are taught known as hell. Today is the only thing that exists to me.

Rick: Okay.

Steven: And I've already accomplished today what I've chosen to do. Tomorrow, if and when that moment arrives, then I'll do that.

But the object that I would truly love to see in the world is to become consciously aware of its own absolute greatness, its own perfection, and its own sacredness.

And treat life in that same fashion. And the only country that negates that happens to be this one, and only because of the need of control.

Rick: Have you ever thought of taking on students and training them the way you were?

Steven: This one. (Referring to Mark.) I haven't. (Starts laughing sarcastically.) You know the funniest people ever to be around are monks, actually as they demonstrate truth in a humorous way.

Rick: What's that?

Steven: Monks. They are the most good-natured people you'd ever want to meet. They are sarcastically humorous.

Rick: I love to be around them.

Steven: They show you constantly, meaning they will mirror everything that you do so that you can see it for yourself.

Rick: Yeah, (laughing), I got no problem with it.

Steven: They are such masters of the seven mirrors of relationship that they can reflect to you who you are, (snaps fingers) that fast. The drop of a hat.

(Mark enters.....some confusion.)

Steven:The founder of InnerCircle Publishing. That's Chad. Rick has his second book about to come out. Which there will probably be four more.

Rick: Four more? That sounds about right.

Chad: What's that?

Rick: He said there's going to be four more books. Actually I thought there'd be a few more than that. But I'll settle with four.

Steven: That's all I'm seeing right now.

Rick: Cool.

Chad: That's a whole interesting question about what's attached to people's energy or what resonates in their energy. So you just immediately sense when you come in contact with people.

Rick: It's a dawning after awhile? After you've been around them for awhile? The energy pervades through and ..... Oh, it's instantaneous?

Steven: Instantaneous is the proper way to view it, but it all appears in Divine Timing.

Rick: Wow.

Steven:(Chuckling.) I've got this gal in Reno who will call me and say: Steven, I've got this new guy. Can you meet me at such and such place?

So I'll show up at (location) and they say, "Steven, this is so and so." "Hey, howya doin'?" Then I walk away. And they'll come over and "Well, what do you think? Get away from this dude?" (All laugh.)

Steven: First time we ever spoke on the phone, I talked with you about you.

Chad: Um hmm. And was right on. Extremely right on.

Steven:I mean, I don't know when it's going to happen. And it's not something you can turn off and on. Its just there.

Rick: When you do your personal sessions with people, what do you do?

Steven: Get naked!! (Everyone laughs.)

Rick: Hey, that could be therapeutic too. I was interested if it was some kind of therapy.

Steven:Yeah, in a way it is, but from an intuitive perspective as I can sense the vents of the past and bring them to the present and show them where it is taking them and why.

Rick: Okay.

Steven: I have people who quite often, in fact I shoulda.... I'm a heck of a blend between a therapist and a psychic.

Rick: Yeah.

Steven: And I don't care for the word psychic.

Rick: Yeah.

Steven: That's why I don't like the word intuitive. I've never been on the other side of what I do. You have. (To Mark.) What would you call it? Insanity at its finest?

Mark: Yeah.

Steven: There you go.

Rick: So, do you have the person discuss his issues? Do you take them into the past?

Steven: Either way. I have no idea what I'm going to do with a person until I'm there. I'll give them the opportunity, me more so than them probably, and then I just ask them, "What do you want to know?"

And then they'll tell me. And then I begin the process. I'll put my hands on them and I'll go into other lifetimes. I can go backwards or forwards. If they want to know about a person on the other side of the planet, if they have a son or a daughter in Iraq, I can follow that and I can tell them what they're doing. There's almost....

Rick: That's an incredible gift. I've seen glimpses of it. But it's not anything I have conscious control over. I can't do it at will.

Steven: Sure you can.

Rick: Well, yeah, I'm sure I can. I'm working towards, you know, being that way.

Steven: It's called openness. It's called being open to whatever, and be flexible with what you sense and do not judge it, as this is the largest stumbling block. Learn to see things as they are, not as they aren't.

You know, a lot of people on the spiritual road are known to be incredible givers. But there is another side to that coin. Even the symbolisms of the story of Christmas have two things going on, not just giving. It's also receiving. The best givers are those that are able to receive. I mean, I went through…um…seven readings today and I don't look tired. And when we were in St. Louis, we had the festivities of all the kids on Friday night.

Mark: That was a long weekend.

Steven: Got up Saturday. Read all day. On Saturday night….no. Read for people all day. Went out to dinner. Did a radio show until midnight. We got back to the hotel at almost one. Got up the next morning. Did two Sunday Services and a three hour channeling session and didn't end it till five. There's no such thing as being drained as long as there's no attachment to it.

Rick: Right.

Steven: And if there's no attachment and no judgment, then you can say anything you want in life. Absolutely.

Rick: (To Mark.) Let me ask you something now. How long have you been a student of Steven's?

Mark: A year.

Rick: A year? Okay. Give us a rundown of what, you know, of how you feel your life has changed.

47

Mark: I guess the biggest thing that I've learned with Steven was that you can be your own enemy and your perception of yourself is not true.

Rick: Yeah.

Mark: Is not always true

Rick: Yeah. I can have a little reality on that one too.

The tape finished one side at this point. While I loaded a new tape, Steven kept talking. We come back to it with him expounding.

Steven: I believe in working *with* Spirit. Religion in and of itself, is because of Emperor Constantine, in his conversion to Christianity, and the only reason he was converted to Christianity and/or really allowed it, is because he realized the significance. If you study the four traditions of Christianity, which is the Marcionites, the Thomasines, the Ebionites, and the Gnostics, the Bible has portions of all four of those paths, and they combined it into the book that we call the Bible.

But if you understand the traditions, the fear factor comes in through the Marcionites and the Ebionites. The Gnostics were the spiritual teachings and the Thomasines or the twin, is the true teachings of what Christ was all about.

And what they did was they took the information from those four versions and combined them into one, burying the rest, including maybe the most important of all, and that's the feminine aspect of the idea of God.

The thing that fascinated me about the Da Vinci code is the idea of the six-pointed star. [That] just took place in an astrological thing that took place on the 11th of November last year, which was the pentagram being formed by all the planets, or the reunion of the masculine with the feminine energy, which is now taking place, that vibration, on the Earth.

Mark: What I think is interesting to see is the dichotomy that the Catholic Church has created, because the Madonna is the classic Goddess.

Chad: The Pagans always worshipped the feminine aspect.

Mark: Now here they created this whole patriarch and in the heart of their patriarch is the Madonna.

Rick: Exactly.

Steven: Actually, prophecy stated that we would return to her.

Rick: And they pray to her like She's a Goddess.

Steven: She is.

Rick: Well, I agree with you, but we're not taught that She is, though. Even though we practice it. You know, She's got everything but the title. (Laughs)

Steven: Well, well, in fact, it was Peter's ego when the ascension happened, um...when Mary was appointed the successor and Peter couldn't handle that. Pope Gregory truly built on this idea to stop Goddess energy, as it was against early church doctrines.

Rick: Right. He was jealous, in fact, of her and I remember reading that in The Book of Thomas, I think it was.

Steven: Yes. And Peter's the one that ended up usurping Mary, and he went to Rome to let them know that the women were attempting to take over the world, which is also an attribute of the Inquisitions again.

Rick: Mmm.. hmm.

Steven: …Which the Pope himself apologized for in 1996.

Steven: The idea of Christ coming in on a cloud, I mean, you'd have to be a monk to actually see it to see what that is and what that means. It's not that Jesus would reappear in the clouds. It's just Jesus would be realized, or Christ Consciousness would be realized within you.

Steven: He told them not to worship idols. And what did they do? They created the external idols that we now worship. God in reality is an internal thing as Jesus Himself stated, and everyone misses because we are taught that we are not worthy.

Rick: They worship idols.

Steven: Mmm hmm. Thanks, pumpkin (to Mark, as he was leaving) (Everyone laughing).

Mark: Sweetpea…

Steven: Ah, you'd never get a date, not that you do now.

Rick: (Bursts out laughing.)

Steven: Neither do I. I just sit at home.

Rick: I don't even want dates, man, I avoid'em (laughing).

Steven: Oh, I love female energy. It is not as hectic as masculine nor as dominant.

Chad: I was going to say that eventually I bet female energy loves you.

Steven: Loves what?

Chad: You.

Steven: When I'm doing a channeling thing while I'm lecturing, it's a different gig for me. It's a different head totally as it has to be open.

Rick: Yeah.

Steven: And I trust the universe so much that I just flat turn it over. When I'm actually doing a channeling thing, with the many energies I work with, I have to quote them mostly verbatim. They do allow me the flexibility to use modern, humanistic terms, except for three of them. They prefer exactness.

Rick: I see.

Steven: And when I'm doing those three, you hear "Thee, thine," and it's right in absolute conversation. Just wham, wham, wham, wham, wham. And I've heard people say, "That's like right out of the Bible." Yes, it appears that way, yet you cannot find it there.

Steven: There was one night that Morya stepped in, because there was this one lady in the back of the room that wouldn't cop to a truth. And all of a sudden - you were there (to Mark) - I stood up and literally waded right through rows of chairs, right at her, and then stood right over her, over the top of her, and just flat got in her face, basically. That's what happened.

Mark: She cut loose and then relaxed, because it appeared she understood.

Rick: What did you have to get in her face about? I'm curious what the subject was.

Steven: When you're...ah...when you're with Spirit, directly, and you're hanging onto your past, and they are showing it to you, because they will, they'll talk with you and show you the different sides and the different attributes just like a diamond. And when that person won't let go and then, Morya's known as the Taskmaster, I mean that energy just comes, "Wham," right down on the person.

Rick: Like a spiritual Sergeant-at-Arms or something?

Steven: Ahhh... "Butt-Kicker" at times is more appropriate.

Rick: Okay.

Steven: Don't deny it.

Rick: Gotcha.

Steven: And it's right there, and if you deny it, he'll walk you right through, not knowing any of the events... will walk you right through what you were going through, and you're sitting there going, "Oh my God, he knows!"

Rick: Uh huh. Got to love that.

Steven: And then it just....oh, no, that's scary. Even to me, it's like, "Holy Smoke!" Because I apologized for a long time.

Rick: Well, I've had that done to me. And it was so humbling, man, I crumbled on the spot and just, you know, confessed everything and I mean I went on for like two hours. I confessed everything in my life! (Laughing)

Chad: Really?

Rick: Yes! I couldn't believe the guy could be in my head like that.

Steven: Absolutely.

Rick: And when he did that, I just went, "Holy cow!"

Steven: It can be anywhere It wants to… spirit or consciousness.

Rick: Huh?

Steven: It can be anywhere It wants to.

Rick: Yes!

Steven: I mean, It can be in any instant. God is a funny thing. And I have no hesitation…there's only one place really, two places, now one, that allowed me to just free rein, knowing absolutely that I'm channeling. This is what he's doing. And you've seen me do it (to Mark.) My voice changes… they shift and change and it could be any one of nineteen.

Rick: Wow.

Steven: Okay? And I could tell you who they are, but they don't like for you to say who is talking to them.

Rick: Yeah.

Steven: And the truth is they'd do it anyway, but…

Rick: I've had some writing experiences I thought were being channeled, but I need to have more experience with it to really know.

Steven: What's channeling to you?

Rick: It's just bringing in knowledge directly from Spirit, really.

Steven: Oh. What's going on with you (when that happens)?

Rick: I have …. there's an openness. And then I start receiving impressions. And I can't honestly say that I'm creating those thoughts myself, because I know when I'm imagining something. I know when I'm putting direct energy into the creation. This is more like a .... an intermingling, a communion. I know it's not all me. But I know that I'm contributing to it.

Steven: It's a ..... layman's terms.

Rick: Um hmm.

Steven: Ah…they are thoughts that are not your own.

Rick: Yeah.

Steven: Watch for thought groups, thought streams, that are not your own.

Rick: Yeah. I pick up on consciousness a lot, and I got to make that differentiation between who's thinking what.

Steven: Yeah. The object of a monk, in a nutshell, is to know how you think, and how your mind operates, what your thought streams are. They are your personality. Okay?

Rick: I'm really starting to tune in on that now.

Steven:(Pauses.) She.

Rick: Stacy?

Steven: Stacy. I was going to say Shelly. Who is that?

Stacy, okay, yeah right. (Laughter). You have your personalities. You have your thought streams that you have been with all of your life. The first key in it is to learn how you think. What do you think when you're thinking? How do you word it in your head? And then ask a question. Make it as

54

abstract as you can make it. Okay? How is the universe put together? I mean something wild.

Rick: Yeah.

Steven: Then what you do is you observe all the thought streams. And you learn to identify the one that you know is not your ordinary thought grouping, the way you word it in your head. I know that sounds as complex as all daylight.

Rick: Its not. I'm digging it completely.

Steven: But its not. It's a piece of cake. Once you get that thought stream that you know is not yours, *that's* the one to listen to.

Rick: Yeah.

Steven: You can determine. There's more to it than that. And then if you watch, instead of what you identify is the way your head operates, and then you may find fifteen different thought streams going on.

[As] every human, you were born with four energies that work with you, and their function is to guide you through the different stages. They change. So, four of those thought streams belong to them.

Rick: Yeah.

Steven:I mean, they'll tell you, "No, don't turn right." But you got to pay attention to it.

Rick: Um hmm.

Steven: Okay? I'm cruising down the highway one day, and I have my headset on listening to a CD. And all of a sudden…this thing in my head said, "Move to your left now."

55

Didn't look. Didn't blink. Moved to the left and then…said now look, and as I was moving, I didn't look behind me. I didn't know if there was a car there. It was open and I looked over, and there was this semi coming over into my lane as if I was not even there, and that was one of the four that came in with me. And when you learn to separate you, you can identify the rest. Anyway, that got off the subject a little bit. It's your fault. (Laughter)

Chad: Yeah, that's perfect.

Mark: Steven, do you have a room key?

Rick: Of course not. (Laughs)

Chad: No, (laughs) he's got it.

Steven: You got your wallet?

Mark: No.

Steven: You don't have your wallet? You don't have any cash on you?

Mark: I got cash. I don't have a room key.

Steven: Oh, cool. What's it worth to you? (Laughter)

Rick: He was working it.

Steven: One of the voices in my head said….(more laughter)

Steven: No, but that's channeling.

Rick: Yeah, okay.

Steven: Every human's done it.

Rick: Then, I've done it.

Steven: Have you ever said something to a person and you didn't know what you said? And they go, "Whoa! What did you just say?" Well, I don't know.

Stacy: (Laughs) I don't know.

Steven: You just channeled that. It's hard for people to imagine. Look, let me ask you a question. Honestly.

Rick: It's a subtle awareness.

Steven: Put yourself in this thing we call God's shoes. All right. And here's what you wanted to do. You wanted every human to be just like you - every physical human. You wanted to give them the whole power of the universe. You wanted them to work for it. You wanted to make it difficult, but not so difficult that nobody would ever find it.

Rick: Right.

Steven: But now your object was to take all this magnificent ability and disguise it. How would you do it?

Rick: Yeah! See, that creates the perfect game for a human being.

Steven: Walk in the park.

Rick: It's a perfect game. It's got mystery. It's got something to gain, something to lose, something to risk, you know?

Steven: Stacy, lovely one, how would you do it?

Stacy: (Laughs) Well, I can't talk right now.

Steven: Try this on. That you make it so simple, and you put it in plain sight, and because it is in plain sight, nobody would buy it.

Rick: Too obvious.

Steven: Because you knew it would be so logical that they would need proof. Wouldn't that, wouldn't that make sense?

Stacy: Yeah.

Rick: Yeah. Yeah, that they would need proof.

Steven: Two keys

Rick: I like that.

Steven: Funny thing about Biblical text. Christ Himself said, "You must have the mind of the child." "You must have the innocence of the child." That's two direct hints, because the innocence of a child would accept the validity and simplicity of it because it could deal with it. But as we become adults our innocence moves away. And it blocks it.

Rick: This is what *Return to Innocence* is about?

Steven: (Smiles) We're getting there. (To Chad) I mean, I think you're right. I put one thing or a point right after the other. I don't give you a break between it. There is no fluff, so it makes it intense and you have to think through what I write.

Rick: No, I like it like that.

Chad: I do too.

Steven: But to me, that's the walk in the park.

Rick: I like it like that. Gets drilled in on me good.

Steven: The fact that...

58

Chad: You can always stop if you need a break or whatever.

Steven: The title of the next book is *What if God Were Your Ego?*. And that's when I'm going to do it, get very intense.

Stacy: (Laughing) Ohhhh…

Rick: What if God were your ego?

Steven: Yeah. Was your ego. Your ego, and your ego.

Stacy: Yeah.

Rick: Oh my God! Please. I would never want to touch God being my ego. God! This planet would be in worst shape than it is now! (Laughing)

Steven: Oh? Really?

Rick: *My* ego?

Steven: I got news for you. It is.

Part IV:

Picking up the pieces

of blown minds

Chad: Yeah.

Stacy: (Laughing)

Rick: It is what? (I can't believe what I'm hearing.)

Steven: Look in my eyes.

Rick: Yeah.

Steven: God is your ego. It is your ego. And it is your ego. And it is my ego.

Rick: This flies directly into....

Steven: I'm going right in your face, and the face of our learned conditioning.

Rick: Well, okay, now I was going to explain. But I'll just listen. I'll just listen.

Steven: So much in ancient texts talk about a duel-edged sword, that it will swing both ways. It can love, it can hate. And you have a choice. We've misinterpreted the ego as an evil, bad thing. Satan, in ancient texts, literally interpreted, is ego.

Rick: Right.

Steven: Misused. God, in ancient texts, is proper-used ego. One thing, one question you have to answer for yourself, will give you the whole answer to the whole thing: What's the creative power in every single human?

Rick: God.

Steven: No, no. Think about it.

Steven: God is three letters. Ego is three letters. E-G-O. G-O-D.

after the D. One notch under human, or God. What gives God life? You do. You do. You do. Did God create us to worship it? Nooooo. You show me anyplace in the Bible where Jesus groveled when He spoke to God. He commanded it.

Jesus may have never been a human. Period. What if Christ is the consciousness that resides within the ego? We must make the two into one. Look at the symbol of yin and yang and the statement "Let there be light". There are two forces originally created, masculine and feminine. They become what we call the ego. But, psychology says the ego is a dangerous, bad thing. A lot of writers today, even in *The Power of Now*, say the ego is dying. What would humans be without the ego? What would they be?

Rick: Powerless.

Steven: They could do nothing. How could you create? Same image and likeness. What does that mean?

Chad: And you will come to know that I am…

Steven:…and I am not.

Rick: Judgment of your ego.

Steven: Okay. And if it's your ego that's doing it, it's a duel-edged sword. And it swings back.

Rick: Now I understand….

(Everybody starting to laugh.)

Chad: Well, there goes that reality.

Steven: Imagine…imagine being around a Monk for six years.

Rick: Yeah. That's what I need to do, see.

Steven: But you know what? Ponder that. Truly. Because in Genesis, it states, "I will make," going to change a word, "human" in My image and likeness. Human.

Rick: God has an ego too.

Steven: If God is not your body then what is it in you that is the image of It? There is only one creative thing in a human and the body executes the creative energy that is produced by that creative force.

Rick: Will? Intent? (I still can't quite integrate this concept yet.)

Steven: It's still the same source.

Rick: Well, yeah. I'd call it spiritual energy.

Steven: It's ego.

Rick: Ego?

Steven: It's your ego. It's every human's ego. Again, it is the creative principle for the human to use in whatever fashion that we so choose.

It's not important to me whether you buy it or not. You want to create? You want to heal? Then learn to wield that. There's nothing else you need to wield other than that.

Everything that a Monk does is focused on you recognizing that power. And it's how you wield it. It can swing either way. You see the imagery in Chinese. You see it in Japanese. You see it in African. Ancient stuff. The symbol of yin and yang is ever present. That's all it means. Two sides of the ego.

What if I were to say to you guys, that if you take the number of the disciples, twelve, and add Mary Magdalene and Jesus, you have fourteen. You cut that number in half you have seven. How many chakras you got? Seven. Each chakra has two sides to the coin. Now you bring in the other seven.

If you look at the acts and the demonstrations symbolically in the Bible, about the disciples, Jesus, and Mary, you'll find an absolute opposite, polarizing force between each of them. The perfect example is Judas/Jesus. Judas, pure physical form, greed, base. Look at this. They both died. One killed itself and the other was killed by that part. Slain by the physical form, to rise again.

Note: At this point there is a break in conversation. The tape recorder is voice activated, and there is some conversation missing as the tape recorder picks back up into recording mode. Steven asked if we knew of Kuthumi. None of us did. As we pick the conversation back up, Steven is telling us about this being.

Steven: This is what the Bible is about.

Chad: That's what the Bible is about?

Steven: Yes sir. Learning to focus your own ego-based, human substance on a single target called a person.

Rick: (Laughing) You know what you're doing? For me, what you are doing is stripping off false data I have been operating from. And by putting the right data there, in front of me, I'm consuming this in large chunks and quantities.

Steven: You have to.

Rick: And... ah...boy, it's... I can feel the... (shifting around)

Steven: Makes you think about a few things.

64

Rick: I've had my whole life flash in front of me here in the last few minutes.

Steven: It's never important whether you agree with what you are learning or not. Be objective and look at it.

Chad: Yeah.

Rick: A lot...

Steven: Remember the first question? (Pause) Just blew your mind, huh, Sweetie? (To Stacy) Sorry about that. First question I asked you: If you were God and you were creating all things and you wanted to create an interest in something you could attain, how would you do that? It would have to be simple, straight-forward, and wide out in the open. And something nobody would look at.

Rick: That would be the last place I would ever look. The last place I would look (referring to the ego as God) Because you know what? I thought I was making huge in-roads lately, because...

Steven: You are. You are.

Rick: ....I was getting to a point where I was actually successfully integrating my ego into my self. But I still had some...some misinformation. You know? I wasn't quite getting it. You know? This makes a lot of sense. Man.

Steven: But you...but you can find it, everything that was said to you, can be found in ancient texts.

Chad: Right.

Steven: You can find it. It's written in the Bible. It's written in the Torah, the Koran, the Kabala.

Rick: I can't …I can't think of how many times since I was a little boy, I'd exercise my power. You're exercising your ego, and someone comes along and convinces you it was wrong.

Steven: Um hmm.

Rick: …that you're hurting others by being that way. And that will cause a being to shut down his power immediately if he thinks he is hurting someone. If he's convinced he's harming someone?

Chad: Sure.

Rick: He'll shut it down.

Chad: Sure.

Rick: This is too good.

Chad: As far as that being written anywhere, what you're saying, you know? I've always, whether I've read something, or listened, or just come in contact with it, however, like when you meet someone and you feel their aura, their energy, you feel them….I've always felt that anything I ask, like you said, any question you ask, and any question gets a response. I'm not intelligent enough to know if the response is accurate, because I don't have that information. All I know is what I see.

Steven: One Corinthians. Remember, Paul says, "Walk in faith, but not necessarily with what the eyes see."

Chad: Right.

Steven: Again, you have to look at something. What's faith? What is that? Faith, or feel is… what's the biggest feeder of ego?

Chad: How you feel?

Steven: What you see. What we see is what someone does. We are either going to agree or disagree with that. But what we're going to do is witness that. The words are being chosen here. Because every word I'm offering you is somewhere in the Bible. Okay?

Chad: Yeah.

Steven: Once it's witnessed, the natural knee-jerk reaction, because of what you see, is the judgment. "This is good, or this is bad."

What if it just is? When you can learn to see life as it just is, it negates what these (the eyes) see. And then you can *see* anything you want to.

So, the Ancients are saying walk in faith, it's saying be aware of what these human tools do. But here's what you saw. And that's what ladies do when you say why women like you. You're a rugged man. You have a sensitivity that ordinarily a rugged man wouldn't have. So women are going to be drawn to that. It's what you feel.

But what maybe…what it doesn't do is walk their high sensitivity. When you walk here, this is God. Ask yourself a question, or another idea, another way to look at it. There are two forces at work, masculine and feminine, as was suggested earlier. We call them positive and negative. And I don't care which way you place the poles, doesn't matter to me. Now you have a life, and it has a positive and a negative charge. You have an ego, a chakra. The representation of the disciples is a positive and a negative charge, or masculine and feminine based representation with Mary and Jesus at the head: the feminine nature in equal harmony with the masculine energy. Masculine. Feminine. It's everywhere that you look. Water: feminine. Land: masculine. Night: feminine. Day: masculine. Clear, warm day: masculine. Cool day, or even cold day: feminine. Add wind to it, you have masculine day with feminine turbulence. Tornado is the same, condensed, controlled force.

So the object is realizing what is the primary energy source of that battery within the human. It still takes you to one place. What do you base your decisions and your judgments from? Up here (in the head) and what the ego deems it. Now you have your Satan and God. It's still your ego. It doesn't matter how anybody looks at it. It comes out the same. The key, though, is to look through the objective side of being and not the subjective side which will create judgement.

Chad: Right.

Steven: This statement here, and this is verbatim. Okay? I don't play with the words on this one. I'll tell you if it's adapted. In fact, this says adapted. But not really. Yeah it is. They took the "man" out. It says "human."

Mark: Oh, yeah.

Steven: "Then shall the human seek peace with their own thoughts, that the Angel of Wisdom may guide them. For I tell you truly, there is no greater power in heaven and earth than the thoughts of the human.

"Though unseen by the eyes of the body, yet each thought has mighty strength as can shake the heavens. For to know every creature in the Kingdom of the Earthly Mother is it given the power of thought. For all beasts that crawl and birds that fly live not of their own thinking but of the one law that governs all.

"Only to the Sons of Men is it given the power of thought. Even that thought that can break the bonds of death. Do not think because it cannot be seen that the thought has no power. I tell you truly, the lightning that cleaves the mighty oak, or the quaking that opens up cracks in the earth, these are as the play of children compared with the power of thought.

"Truly each thought of darkness, whether it be of malice, anger, vengeance, these reap destruction like that of fire

68

sweeping through the dry kindling under a windless sky. The human does not see this carnage. Nor do they hear the piteous cries of their victims as they are blind to the world of spirit.

"Yet when this power is guided by higher wisdom then the thoughts of the Sons of Men lead them to the heavenly kingdoms and thus is paradise built on earth. Then, it is that your thoughts uplift the souls of humans as the cool waters of a rushing stream revive your body in the summer heat." Circa, 500 B.C.

Rick: (Laughing)

Steven: That says it all.

Chad: Yeah.

Rick: No kidding.

Steven: People will read that and go, "Horse hockey." Even if it's flippant (the thoughts), there's no take-backs. You can't uncreate. You can only create just like what we call God, for that is what It does, and we are in Its image and likeness. It's all you can do. How do you create and what's going to do that? It leads you to the same point. And already realizing and knowing that God isn't located some place geographically, so where in heavens name is it? Nobody has ever really paid attention.

Rick: It's everywhere.

Steven: Yes, indeed it is. All things are God created, so therefore we are the same as It is.

Rick: Everywhere around us, within us, above us, below us.

Steven: Gospel of Phillip in the Nag Hammadi: "When you lift the rock you find me there. When you split the wood you find me there. When you carry the water you find me there."

Still, there's one power behind it. Why do you think we have life? You, me, and you? It's all about two energies, two forces.

Rick: Ummm…what happened to Mark?

Steven: Ah…He probably, um…. died. (Laughter)

He took the key from me so I can't get in. (More laughing)

Note: We took a short break to find Mark.

Steven: If that didn't make any sense, again I apologize.

Rick: Oh, no. What it dragged my attention to here is, and I'm going to tell you about this, is…

Steven: Oh oh.

Rick: ….you know this thing about having these bad thoughts worries me, because, try as I have tried to not have them, I've had them and my main target is my ex-wife because she's the most recent (disaster) here and whatever. And I catch myself doing it and, man, I've just got to collect it. And then I go, well, see, it's already too late. You know? How do you get around all that? I honestly don't mean her any harm. But, there's still those uncontrolled thoughts. I don't know how to stop having them.

Steven: Well, you can look at it this way. When you think those things you're actually pointing at you.

Rick: Yeah, and I get all of that. I get all of that. I get mad at myself….

Steven: Which is what Jesus meant when He said: when you strike your enemy, you're basically hitting you.

Rick: Yeah.

Steven: I think Buddha said that, actually. Jesus said when your enemy hits you on one cheek, offer them the other also. Then tell them to F.O. Which is just "Fun Outside." So that's no big deal.

Stacy: (Laughs)

Rick: Yeah. But you know, I hate having thoughts like that, you know? Those aren't the thoughts that people like me, who has the goals that I have, those aren't thoughts that a person like me should be entertaining.

Steven: I can't tell you how to think, but I can state that what you resist persists. You see, if we choose to have a different outcome, then we simply create different choices.

Rick: I'm not telling…I'm not asking how to think. What I am pointing out is that, try as I may to stop having them, you still have them. I don't like that. I have them. I scold myself over it. I try to separate, because I realize that it's not good.

Steven: Who would you say, if you were to pick, who would you say are the most focused humans you can think of?

Rick: Most mentally focused humans?

Chad: As a race, as a people?

Steven: Eh. All three of you know the answer already.

Rick: Oh, well, Jesus.

Chad: Monks.

Steven: Yeah, the Monks.

Rick: Monks, right.

Steven: They're taught to do that.

Chad: Right.

Steven: Where do they teach you to do that, other than in a monastery? That's the reason we're here, if you really want to know. How to think. Silly analogy. What if every human, all of a sudden their arms flailed, and they didn't know when? How often would you drive a car? (Laughter) How often would you shop? How often would you do anything? Because you never know when these (arms) are going to start flapping. (More laughter) Right? So, why do you do it in your head? You control this. But what's doing it? It's your ego, focused. It's your option to think about your ex-wife. You're going to run into a telephone pole while staring at the highway behind you. That's living back there. If you have a hate, an anger, or a frustration with anything back there, that part of you is now bound there and stuck in time, this is the idea of Lot's wife. You can have all the desire to progress forward spiritually, but as long as you got all these anchors back there, you aren't going anywhere. That's like having three master sails into the wind and the boat is still tied to the pier. (Laughing) Something's going to give.

Rick: Well, I've struggled with this a lot and Chad knows, because I've opened up and told Chad about this quite a bit. And.....

Steven: Change what you think.

Rick: Yeah, I know.

Steven: If you think for a second that somebody's a nincompoop, you're going experience being that. And as long as you have your focus on your anger at your ex, it's because, in reality, there's still a heck of a chunk of you that loves her that you'd rather cover under dirt, which gives you a reason to hate her.

Rick: No. I ....

Steven: Ah ah.....

Rick: Okay, I'll shut up. (Laughing)

Steven: Um...One of the things, when you first become a Monk, is how well does the individual hear? And that includes all the faculties.

No, it's not that specific girl. My point is love, for you, is under the dirt of anger. It's the point. And it's easier to say, "Well, you did this to me."

There's seven things known as the seven Essene mirrors. The first one is what's going on in the moment. But there's lost love, I think it's number four, which means what agony or what pain do you have that holds you away from the ideal of what the concept of love is. So, for you there's a lot of grays in here, because you're still angry at her, and this will show every time you decide that you love another. You're angry at her because maybe she didn't love you in return. But keep in mind that has nothing to do with her. It's you. Are you with me?

Rick: Yes.

Steven: All right. You should hear that it's not her. It's the lack of the sense of love within you that you don't have that she may have taken, crushed, harmed, dashed, whatever. If we learn to focus on that, on the positive nature of the pole....look, you can't deny ugly thoughts because they grow. And who'd want to deny beautiful stuff. Ugly things are one of the poles. Beautiful stuff's... I love the beautiful stuff...(laughter). The beautiful stuff is the positive pole.

Now, where are you putting your energy? It's on the ugly stuff. And you've totally forgotten this. Again, that's the ego, because it has the two sides. Ego, the four principles of

73

the ego, it wants you to grow old, it wants you to fail, it wants you to die, and it wants you to get sick.

Rick: And yet, it's God.

Steven: Yes! Because you have the choice of how you operate with God, which is why I said to you earlier, Christ never groveled. He knew how to operate with God. He only saw one thing. It's all over the place. You can't serve two masters. You can't be good and you can't be bad. If you worship this, you can't have that. But it always says you're in the driver's seat.

Mark: (Laughs) Yeah, that's right, it always does.

Steven: And it's up to you which way you turn the car. I don't know why, ah...you know. Other than that, people are always floored when I do this with them. But it's the truth, and I've never gone this far with it in public. And I don't know if I would. I will. But I am going to at some point. Because if you really think about it, even in a logical sense, I've answered every logical question you have. I've answered every emotional question you have. And every time I've brought you right back into balance with it. Because that's the way it works. It's that simple.

You have the choice, my friend. Every human, they'll look at you and go, "What, you think you're perfect?"

You have your vision. You have your choices. You can choose what you wish. And that has no business on me. So, whichever you choose me to be, I'll accept it. How do you answer that? You don't. You don't even mess with it. (Everyone laughing)

Chad: It's a rhetorical mouse trap. I mean....(laughing)

Steven: It's true. Because you can see me however you choose and it's the same as me seeing you, you, you...

Chad: Sure.

Steven:… You, your ex-wife. Where, where are you putting the charge? You put it on both so you can operate the battery. Both exist. Both have life. But this is what you want. Love, peace, harmony, joy, abundance, for the whole darn thing. Let's do it. And use this and this, and make it. Use this ugly stuff and this good stuff, and make something cool, by not judging it, and allow for both sides of the coin, and learn to see things as they are instead of as they are not. Only being objective will allow this to take place and nothing less.

Rick: Yeah.

Chad: Exactly.

Steven: Make sense? That's your ego.

It still comes back to the same point. There's no way around it. And this man can look at you as a Monk, as a person. I've enjoyed you all even though I just met you all and blown your minds (chuckling), but that's cool. Ask your own self. Let your own self show you how it all works. And it will. Because it's unique to you.

Boy, you guys just got four years of "Monkdom" in about an hour.

Chad: And it's amazing because, what I was saying before is what you're saying I can feel. Every time I've ever listened to a politician or somebody else….no, I mean anybody, a guy on the street, when he's talking to me, I know how full of it he really is. I can smell it. And I feel how much of it is for real or not. And everything you're saying …..

Steven: Sounds right.

Chad: Exactly. Exactly.

Steven: But you know something? There is no right or wrong.

Chad: I can understand that part of it too.

Steven: Okay.

Chad: But you put it in a way that...

Steven: It's something to get out there with strangers. I think everything in my life always pointed me to focus and the ability to stay that way.

Rick: Yeah. That's just one I'm just not ready for. I think in other lifetimes I've done plenty of it and I'm just sick of it.

Steven: Yeah, everybody in this room has.

Chad: Really?

Steven:Sure.

Chad: Just because everybody has or...

Steven: I was given a number when I was staying with the Zens. And I was given the exact same number by the Tibetans almost five years later. First one I shined on. Second time... the number I was given was how many times I've been here. 1,176 times.

Chad: Here in the monastery with them?

Steven: Here. As a human.

Rick: How many lifetimes.

Steven: 1,176.

Chad: Can you tell, or can you....

Steven: Yeah, I know exactly.

Chad: With other people?

Steven: Sure.

Chad: Really?

Steven: Yeah.

Rick: How many do you feel coming out of me?

Steven: Oh, I don't know. I'd have to focus on you for a bit. (Looks intently at me)

Off the cuff I've got 390. The average is 200 to 250, is the average. A Down's Syndrome child is a first generation experience.

Rick: Really. I always wondered about that.

Steven: They don't know how to operate the body. Each lifetime is about perfecting your knowledge to create your physical form,or have your physical form match your knowledge,which comes from your experience.

That's what DNA is. You have four memories. You have your conscious memory, which is your conscious mind. You have your subconscious memory, which both of those are known. One of the newest ones they're realizing is cellular memory. That's what athletics is realizing. Guess what the other one is. Your Book of Life happens to be your DNA strain. That's your ancient memory. Physical form is a compilation of these memories, which is why we deal with the past so much. Even in every present lifetime. That's part of the paradox. But when you learn to not focus on it, the past life is a non-issue.

If you look at someone and you say, "Do you realize that you were born last time in 1907?"

"Really? Well, who was I?" "You were Adolph Hitler."

What a crumbler. You weren't. But if you see that in a person, how do you tell them that? Because you can see some pretty wild stuff on a human from an intuitive perspective. All of this is possible when one moves away from their perceived limitations imposed by our learning condition, and this is not very flexible. The reason for this is something that we call being normal and today we all desire to be normal. How is that possible? It is as though we are all supposed to be exactly alike and that is not possible. We are all unique unto ourselves in every aspect.

Buddah. One morning he saw all of his, under the banyan tree, all of his lifetimes. And all of them in that moment became one. And he doesn't get hung up on any previous experience. He's willing to see them all. And you're shown them all, constantly.

Your journey is unique to you. Only you. When he would be asked to explain enlightenment, he always fell silent. Why? If I define enlightenment for you, he's telling you his experience, which would limit you to his experience. So he never defined it.

The Book of Revelations is actually a road map on how to access every past life you've had. The Seven Seals of the Book of Life. You can break them. But you ought to look back. The Apostles and their representation. It's both those forces again, balancing the two. They must have mutual power. That's the sum total of why we do it. If you have a past life that's got you hung? You want to know why you don't see them? Simple. Again, because if you've been here 399 now, then what you'd be seeing is births and deaths. And which one are you in? You have to be in this one. It's a protection device. Built in. If you have one you're hung on, fix it.

Chad: How?

Steven: You feel no shame. Look, I've been a Viking. I've been a pirate three times. Been a monk nineteen. You do it all.

Rick: There's been lifetimes I've viewed where I've slaughtered people. I've done every mean, rotten, nasty, suppressive, murderous, everything that I hate in humanity now I have been or done at some point.

Steven:This is why you hate it today, because you now know the difference.

Rick: Yes. Exactly.

Steven: Good point. Do you believe in no coincidence, no accidents?

Rick: Yes.

Steven: Okay. Where's the mistake? Where's the failure?

Chad: (Laughing)

Rick: Right.

Steven: Where's the issue?

Rick: Right.

Steven: All you can do is get that rested in your own head.

Rick: Right.

Steven: You can't screw up. God would not make a mistake.

Rick: Yeah. That's a hard thing to overcome.

Steven: Okay. But you're doing it.

Rick: Lot of habit.

Steven: Okay. But you're still God.

Rick: I agree.

Steven: Okay. You either are or you are not. I AM or I AM NOT. The ego will put you on I am or it will put you on I am not. It doesn't matter which. But it will do one or the other.

Rick: Well, both of us agree with the I AM thing, I think. Let me take a look. Yeah, we all agree I AM. (General laughing)

Steven:That's all that means.

Rick: I am?

Steven: To further this idea, if you want the literal interpretation, the three parts of a human reaching out with open arms to God, which the ego blocks. This is the idea behind the Om symbol which is on my newest book and all through it in fact.

Rick: Oh wow. Cool.

Steven: I talk too much. I'm going to bed.

All: Thanks a lot Steven.

Parting thoughts....

Well, so there you go. Guys walking on water, making their bodies disappear and reappear, lighting up rooms with no light, living hundreds of lifetimes and generally creating all kinds of havoc with people's ideas of what the hell is really going on here. I always felt in my gut that those things could be done and here, I finally found someone who will admit to it. He has seen it and done it through the teachings found in the Far East, and he is attempting to share this with the American mind set.

Unless you have entertained these ideas, and I would assume that you have or you would have pitched this book long ago as rubbish, this would all seem too bizarre to even consider. And yet so many things point to the fact that all of it, and more, is true and more importantly, obtainable. Perhaps we are so powerful in our thoughts that the slightest thought that we can't prevents us from obtaining those states.

So, in parting, let me leave you with one question: If all of your dreams and ideas of who you are really are what you hope they are, what are you waiting for?

So long for now.

Chad Lilly and Rick LaFerla

Dr. Hairfield can help you in your quest. He has written two books.

The first is *"Once Upon a Parable – a Journey into Life"*. It will answer the questions you may have about the meaning of the Bible, in a metaphysical sense, and it will introduce you to the wonderful spiritual teachings of Eastern philosophies.

His second book is called *"Return to Innocence – Messages from the Ancients"*. Why do we populate the earth? How did it all happen, and how have we shaped our individual and collective destinies? Where do we stand today, and what can we do about it?

Both these books are highly recommended reading if you are interested in your spiritual well-being.

Visit Dr. Hairfield's website for additional information.

www.hairfield.com

INNERCIRCLE PUBLISHING

InnerCircle Publishing: Metaphysical. Poetry. Spiritual. Aware. Philosophical. Insightful. Uplifting. Life Changing. Mind-altering. Informative. Intangible. Honest. Unity. Conductive to elements that align the body, soul, and mind to listen to conscience.

Catalog of Original Titles

Once Upon a Parable by Dr. Steven Hairfield
Return to Innocence by Dr. Steven Hairfield
A Day in the Mind by Chad Lilly
uncommon sense by Chad Lilly
the voice~a metaphysical journey by Rick LaFerla
On the Edge of Decency by Rick LaFerla
100 Keys to the Kingdom by Prince Elven Camp Jr.
Stress Fractures by Andrew Lewis
Life Rhymes by Rene Ferrell
*Handwriting on the Wall-I*CP Anthology
Falling Awake by Royal Atman
The Divine Plan by Vicki Fletcher
Because Why? The Journey Once Asked by Kirstie Silk
Poetry to Touch the Heart and Soul by Marla Wienandt
The Sometimes Girl by Lisa Zaran
Peace Knights of the Soul by Jon Snodgrass, Ph.D.

Order more books from our website

From the Writer to the Reader
www.innercirclepublishing.com

Printed in the United States
67691LVS00001B/52

9 780972 008037